Deep Thoughts

Susan Langdon Clark

BookLeaf Publishing

Incia | USA | UK

Presentation by *BookLeaf Publishing*

Web: www.bookleafpub.com

E-mail: info@bookleafpub.com

ISBN: 9789358315875

First edition 2024

*For Ron, Terry, Joe, Jon, and the many others
whom I love.*

ACKNOWLEDGEMENT

I am grateful for good English teachers all along the way, and I am thankful to be involved in a love affair with the written word.

PREFACE

This book of poetry reveals the life of a marriage gone wrong, the life of a good friendship made at work, and the love of a mother for her children. While it may seem to ramble, it may make perfect sense to some, and that is the best I can hope for.

Not Just for Today

I met him in March of '92.
Our work paths crossed along the way.
Now he has become a good friend
And not just for today.

Somehow we became so close,
The why I've never known,
We were so different, him from me,
In size, in sex, in home.

And yet our minds just thought alike,
In sync, so open and free.
No binding limits, no fakey games,
Between my friend and me.

Always kind and ever true,
Even in the trying times.
I could always see the care
In his reflective eyes.

So often we make acquaintances
As we plod along the way,
So rare it is we make a friend
That's not just for today.

Jerry

Note to reader: In the early 90's, AIDS was a guaranteed death sentence. Jerry lived with it while we traveled for our work assignments.

It was in Madison when he told me the exact nature of his illness.
Until then I could only speculate.

But there, at Wendy's Restaurant, he spelled it out for me
It was not a pretty picture; AIDS was not a pretty picture.

He wanted me to know, he said, in case we were in an auto accident.
Dont touch him, he said. And be sure the medics wear gloves.

That night, and for the next several, sleep did not come easily.
It seemed such a terminal, fatal, predestined ending to a good life.

He gave me no details of how he got it, and I
didn't ask.
I just felt privileged when he let me in on his
"little secret".

At Merrillville in a McDonald's I learned how he
got his death sentence.
Until then, I could only speculate.

He had a hard time telling me. I told him he
didn't have to say it.
I really made no difference; I admired him
anyway.

But he said he had to tell me, so with a blushing
face he told me he was gay.
He wanted me to know, he said, because without
that knowledge a piece of his puzzle was
missing.

That night and for the next several nights, sleep
avoided me.
His life style was such a different one than I had
ever known.

Two years later our friendship has deepened, and
still I worry for him.

The conversation from Madison to Merrillville
haunt the caverns of my mind, and the warmth
of his friendship fills my heart.

On the Road with Jerry

He calls my hotel room, and off we go
Out to eat or off to a show.
Or off to work, we share a car,
Or maybe out to the hotel bar.

We have partied rowdily,
We have laughed and played.
But we have signed and cried some, too.
That's how a friendship's made.

His problems became mine as well,
His depression is mine, too.
It hurts me so to just not know
How I can help him through.

So I just pray and close my eyes
And try to miss his tears.
I just forge on and plunge ahead
While he sits tight in fear.

He knows that death is his reward,
For passion, pure and sweet.
He knows his days are limited,
His Maker he will soon meet.

Some day we'll no longer be
On the road together.
He'll go away and I'll go on,
But in thought we'll be forever.

He will quit work, and volunteer
To help others in his plight,
And I'll go on and work alone,
And miss him every night.

The trips will never be the same,
He cannot be replaced.
The fun we had was aptly clad
By Jerry's smiling face.

I'm not sure how I feel about him.
I hold him deeply as a friend, and love him as a
brother.
And yet our closeness transcends the spoken
word,
Almost as would a lover.

Jerry Was Not at Work

You were not at work today.
You were not sick, but just away.

No morning break to watch you smoke,
And share some thoughts or silly jokes.

No lunch hour friend to go outside
And feel the wind on our backsides.

No PM break to walk around
And find a bench to sit right down.

When you're away my days go wrong.
Get yourself back where you belong!!!

Two as One

Two spirits unemcumbered
by social mores and ideals
Soar side-by-side and evenly
Each knowing what is real.

How can souls so different
Blend today as one?
How does each soul know
The other understands him so?

Near, so near, they soar
Then dip their wings in sync,
Then take flight up high again,
On wings of crystal ice.

The spirits rest together
And talk of everything,
Then sit silently in thought
Souls merged, hearts light.

Knowing sweet contentment,
Feeling total love,
The souls fly off to wonder
How two hearts became just one.

Jerry

He seems so strong, so healthy looking,
So in love with life.
His smile is bright and prevalent,
Though death may soon be calling.

He does not know how long he'll last,
Or exactly when he's going.
He only knows this will not pass,
He cannot get around it.

He eats good meals and takes his pills
And treats his body well.
But one quick fling of unsafe sex
Has caused his own undoing.

He has taught me much, this dying man.
A man I'll love forever.
When he's gone, I will carry on,
Heart heavy, but much smarter.

Jerry is Gone Now

I know he's gone to Paradise,
For one so good as he
Can only sit on clouds of white,
And bow at Jesus' knee.

Somehow I know he's watching me,
As I fill up my days.
Someday again I'll talk to him,
In much the same old way.

We'll discuss how life once was
On the earth below,
We'll smile and talk and laugh a lot
As we once did, long ago.

Only then we'll know the mysteries
Of why things happened so,
And why he died of a dread disease,
And why he had to go.

And why I stayed behind alone,
To continue my life's work.
And why he every crossed my path
To me, on loan from God.

The few years that I had him
Were so full, so warm.
I would not trade them double
Save to keep him safe from harm.

He's gone, but not forgotten,
His voice a memory
Of days of gold enchantment,
A friend he always be.

My Husband and My Life

Some days so close
A sheet of paper could not slide between our
spirits.

Some days apart
Like the crevice made by a small earthquake.

But always parallel and never straying,
Never branching one from the other.

Always rejoining, so close that
A sheet of paper could not slide between us.

Ode to a Lonely Housewife

I am in my kitchen washing dishes while my
friend is in California,
working in James Garner's bank.

I am slipping little shoes on my son's little boy
feet,
 while my friend dons a party dress for a night
on the town.

I am warming tv dinners, while she dines on
wine and steak.
I sleep in a faded gown, while her penoir is lace.

I have slept with the same man for 2,923 days,
while she has a new lover every few weeks.

I kiss my husband goodnight, and sleep comes
easily,
While my friend wonders about the future and
cries herself to sleep.

The Deathknell

The clock strikes one,
Our lives begun.
The clock strikes two,
And where are you?
The clock strikes three,
You're back with me.
As it bongs four
You slam the door.
As it rings five,
I ponder life.
As it rings six,
Our love still sticks.
As it rings seven,
You go on to heaven.
The clock strikes eight,
I was too late.
As it bongs nine,
My death seems fine.
I hear ten chimes,
Then shoot two times,
I never hear eleven.

The King of England

The night is dark, the sky all black.
The cool breeze sends shivers down my back.
The hoot owl hoots, the old cats howl,
As stealthily around her yard I prowl.

I climb a tree to get a peek
Of her fresh beauty, pale and sweet.
The branch shakes, then settles back,
And I peek in the tiny shack.

The coals provide a welcome heat
As she sits near to warm her feet.
Her fine long hair streaks down her spine,
Oh, Tonja, how I yearn to make you mine!

I watch now, as she prepares for sleep.
She combs her golden tresses, the door knob her
garments keep.
Oh, would that I could give her love with fine
and dainty trinkets,
But this cannot be my country thinks,
For I am King of England.

So every night I come here
to this courtyard so far,

And from this tree I watch her sleep,
My Tonja, my fair star.

Thoughts of an Overweight Woman Who Must Travel for Her JobUpon Traveling for My Job

I sit here now, but think of home
And where my family's sleeping.
I watch the jets both land and fly
And wonder why I said goodbye.

I do not like the aloneness that fills this hotel
I sorely miss the happiness that in my home does dwell.
My husband is so kind and good,
My children mostly laughing, as they should.

I am too bashful to enter a dining room alone,
Because the beautiful ladies have companions.
So I eat three candy bars and buy a puzzle book.
And rush back into Room 326.

I am intelligent, they tell me,
But also I am ill.
I need to do something, they say,
And yet, I repeat another day.

How can I do something I am not programmed
to do?
Where can I turn?
It is not to large hotels with lounges like "The
Tree House"
with skinny girls in leopardskin tights.
It is not to a busy, sick and bankrupt husband,
Who needs support himself.
It is not to two young men who cannot yet solve
their own issues,
But it cannot be to a color tv
and a locked hotel room door.

The Boarding House

This is a respectable boarding house,
No traveling salesmen allowed.
No men with small black cases,
No men with lecherous faces
Can slumber with this inn crowd.

This is a respectable boarding house
No dance hall girls need enter.
No girls with long red tresses,
No broads with low-cut dresses,
Can sleep with this inn crowd.

This is a respectable boarding house,
With the straightest folks allowed.
Just men who look straight ahead,
Just women who are prudes in bed
Can reside with this inn crowd.

A Mother's Lament as The Last Child Turns 18

Tonight we're sad, both Dad and me.
Our babe's grown up,
and now, you see,
We soon shall be alone.

She came to us so soft and warm,
An angel from the loft of Heaven.
We loved her so, God only knows,
The joy that she has given.

Today

I climbed a hill
And shopped the town.
I baked a cake,
All nice and brown.
I hummed a tune
And said a prayer,
And mended all the underwear.

Snow

Soft white snow flakes,
Like down from great white birds.
Fluttering softly downward
To lie upon the earth.

I look out through my window
To the mountains snowy white,
And see the flakes come falling
As silent as the night.

Mother is Left Alone

She sits there by the window
Hands folded in her lap.
Her head nods now so slightly.,
She's taking her afternoon nap.

Her eyes that now are faded
Are closed in sweet repose.
She's dreaming of the years gone by
With all their joys and woes.

Of the days when all her babies
Gathered close around her knees
And asked her for a story,
Which she told them just to please.

Now some have gone over Yonder
The rest have married, and gone
To homes of their own, here and yonder,
And mother is left alone.

The Magnificent Sea

There is something about the sea that brings out
the loneliness in me,
And makes my spirit restless.
When I see the waters form white waves and
hear the noise of the sea
As it rebounds on the beaches, I panic.

The magnificent sea, with its eternalness, its
greatness, is free
And I sense that I am not.
I am trapped by the bounds of social conformity,
yet the sea
Knows no conformity at all.

It is free to wander at its will, and can exceed its
boundaries
If that becomes its wishes.
A calm sea can change to an ocean of disaster
and rage
Without fear of imprisonment or shame.

Thanksgiving in Indiana

Apples red, apples golden.
Pumpkin pies and such.
Harvest is here and that doth mean
Guests I love so much.

One good mother, one fine dad,
Three good brothers, dear.
Two sisters sweet will come to eat,
Yes, they'll all be here.

First comes Dad, the head of house,
Who gave us all his seed.
With love enough, he was always there,
To fill my every need.

And Mother Dear, so kind and sweet,
Who always understands me.
She never doubts, but always trusts me.
She has patience more than I, this humble
Mother she.

Then in she comes, this sister dear
Who giggles like a teen.
She still can all my troubles bear,
As we struggle to get lean.

One country sister who loves the land
Now in our midst arriving.
She is priceless for helping out
When there is trouble hiding.

One brother mine is so thin and fine,
My stoutness really shames me,
But he is kind and never minds
that I am fat and homely.

In comes another, a wise big brother
Who seems to speak my language.
I would match his wit with all the lot,
Of Yale, Harvard, and Cambridge.

Then comes in one I love so much,
A friend as well as brother.
He leads a very simple life
And I'd give him my last warm cover.

And so we now all gather,
All of us once more.
In my old orange kitchen
With some folks flowing out the door.

We pray and ask God's guidance
On this family whole.
We pray that He will bless us,
Our hearts, our minds, our souls.

Our Love

Strolling down the seaside, the sky so blue
above,
Reminds me when we were only sweethearts, so
very much in love.

Along the sandy beaches, the tides come rolling
in,
The glittering stars above me tell me our love
will never end.

It took a part of both of us, we made it with our
will.
Our hopes and dreams have truly been fulfilled.

Our love is greater than the dep blue sky.
It belongs to only us. that is the why.

So recall what it says in these few little rhymes,
Our love will only grow with the passage of
time.

From Restless River to Angry Sea

Roll on, oh restless river
As you flow swiftly to the sea.
Frothing, foaming, surging onward,
With a gurgling sound of glee.

Rush on, oh madcap river,
Ever onward toward the sea,
Making foam on wavelets, dancing,
Trying to keep up with thee.

Beat on the shore,
Oh wild angry sea.
Pound the gray stones that
Reach out to thee.

Run over the sands as
A huge, pawing beast,
Panting and frothing,
Oh angry, demonic sea!